333

Phrasal Verbs

We All Must Know

(For All English Learners)

Coach Moin Khan

Amazing Institute of Training and Development

What is a Phrasal Verb?

A phrasal verb combines a verb with an adverb or a preposition to create new verbal phrase—known as the phrasal verb.

What is used for phrasal verb?

Phrasal verbs are phrases that indicate actions. They are generally used in spoken English and informal texts.

Coach Moin Khan

AUTHOR | COACH | MASTER TRAINER

Let's Begin

1-11

1	**Back Down**	*To withdraw your position in a fight, argument, plan, etc.*
2	**Back Off**	*When you leave an emotional situation, or to allow someone to handle something alone.*
3	**Back Up**	*To walk or drive a vehicle backwards.*
4	**Believe In**	*To feel confident about something or someone.*
5	**Blow Away**	*When the wind moves an object or person from where it was.*
6	**Blow Up**	*To make something explode.*
7	**Boil Down To**	*To have determined or analysed the solution or reason for something.*
8	**Break Down**	*When someone loses self-control and is emotionally and/or mentally agitated. This meaning has a noun form for a situation where someone loses self-control.*
9	**Break In**	*To enter a place illegally and with the use of force.*
10	**Break Off**	*To remove a part of something with force.*
11	**Break Out**	*To escape from a place, situation or way of life.*

12-22

12	**Break Through**	*To make a way through a barrier or a surface.*
13	**Break Up**	*To stop a fight.*
14	**Bring Back**	*To return something you've borrowed.*
15	**Bring Over**	*To bring someone or something from one place or area to another.*
16	**Bring Up**	*To bring something from a lower level/place to a higher level/place.*
17	**Brush Off**	*To remove something (dust particle, insect, etc) with your hand.*
18	**Brush Up**	*To practice and review your knowledge or a skill that you haven't used in a while.*
19	**Bump Into**	*When you meet people by accident or unexpectedly.*
20	**Burn Down**	*When someone uses fire to destroy a structure.*
21	**Burn Out**	*When a candle stops burning because there is nothing left to burn.*
22	**Burst Out**	*To suddenly do or say something.*

23-33

23	**Call Back**	*To call someone again.*
24	**Call In**	*To request that someone come and help.*
25	**Call Off**	*To cancel an event that has been previously planned.*
26	**Call Up**	*To be chosen to take part in a military mission.*
27	**Calm Down**	*To become less violent, nervous, excited or angry.*
28	**Care For**	*To nurture or take care of someone or something.*
29	**Carry Away**	*To do something out of the ordinary due to strong emotions.*
30	**Carry On**	*To continue doing something or to continue on in life despite an obstacle.*
31	**Carry Out**	*To move something or someone from one place to another using your arms or an object.*
32	**Catch Up**	*To move faster to reach someone or something that is ahead of you.*
33	**Cheat On**	*When you are emotionally and/or sexually unfaithful to your girlfriend/boyfriend or spouse.*

34-44

34	**Check In**	*To register at a hotel or airport upon arrival.*
35	**Check Out**	*To leave a hotel or other form of an accommodation after your stay there.*
36	**Chop Up**	*To cut something into pieces with a knife.*
37	**Clear Out**	*To remove things completely from an area or place.*
38	**Clear Up**	*To do something to solve a problem or a misunderstanding.*
39	**Close Down**	*When the activities or services of a business permanently end.*
40	**Close Off**	*To block an entrance or pathway.*
41	**Come About**	*When something happens or occurs.*
42	**Come Across**	*The way other people perceive something or someone.*
43	**Come Apart**	*When something breaks or separates piece by piece.*
44	**Come Back**	*To return to a place.*

45-55

45	**Come Down**	*To move from a higher to a lower position or from north to south.*
46	**Come Out**	*To leave a place.*
47	**Come Over**	*To make a visit.*
48	**Come Through**	*When someone or something expected arrives.*
49	**Come Up**	*When something appears or happens, either expected or unexpected.*
50	**Come Up With**	*When you think of a solution, idea, plan, or excuse.*
51	**Con Into**	*To persuade someone to do something through lies and deception.*
52	**Con Out Of**	*To persuade someone to give or do something through lies and deception.*
53	**Cool Off**	*To lose temperature.*
54	**Count On**	*To rely on someone for support when you need it most.*
55	**Count Up**	*To count all of something or people in a group.*

56-66

56	**Cover Up**	*To use something to conceal something else.*
57	**Crack Down**	*To take more action than usual against wrongdoing.*
58	**Cross Off**	*To remove or delete someone or something from a list.*
59	**Cut Back**	*When you spend less money on something.*
60	**Cut Down**	*To do less of something or to use something in smaller amounts.*
61	**Cut Off**	*To completely remove or separate a part of something by cutting it with something sharp like a knife or a pair of scissors, etc.*
62	**Cut Out**	*To remove something using a knife or a pair of scissors.*
63	**Cut Up**	*When you use a knife or scissors to cut something into several pieces.*
64	**Deal With**	*When you do everything, you must do to solve a problem or complete.*
65	**Do Away With**	*To dispose of something.*
66	**Do Over**	*To do something again in order to improve or correct mistakes.*

67-77

67	**Doze Off**	*To go to sleep unintentionally.*
68	**Dress Up**	*To wear formal clothes, or a costume for a special occasion.*
69	**Drop In**	*To visit someone unexpectedly or without making arrangements first.*
70	**Drop Off**	*To gradually decline/become less.*
71	**Drop Out**	*To quit a school program or training course.*
72	**Dry Off**	*To dry something or a surface quickly.*
73	**Dry Up**	*When all the liquid and/or moisture evaporates.*
74	**Eat Up**	*When someone consumes all their food.*
75	**End Up**	*The end result of something planned or unplanned.*
76	**Fall Apart**	*When something breaks all at once or piece by piece.*
77	**Fall Behind**	*To move slower than others.*

78-88

78	**Fall Down**	*To fall to the ground.*
79	**Fall For**	*When you have an intense attraction to something or someone.*
80	**Fall Off**	*When something drops to a lower level.*
81	**Fall Out**	*To fall from or through something.*
82	**Fall Over**	*When someone or something falls from an upright position to the ground.*
83	**Fall Through**	*If things do not go as planned, or if a plan, deal or agreement fails.*
84	**Feel Up To**	*When you have/don't have the energy and confidence to do something.*
85	**Fight Back**	*When you defend yourself/resist an attack, or make an effort against an opponent in a competition.*
86	**Figure On**	*To expect or plan for something.*
87	**Fill In**	*To add personal information in the blank spaces of an official document.*
88	**Fill Out**	*To complete a form.*

89-99

89	**Fill Up**	*To fill something completely.*
90	**Find Out**	*To become aware of something or someone.*
91	**Fix Up**	*To make plans or arrangements with someone or for others.*
92	**Float Around**	*When an object or a person is near, but you cannot pinpoint the exact location.*
93	**Follow Up**	*To find out more about something, or take further action in regards to it.*
94	**Fool Around**	*To waste time doing unimportant or silly things.*
95	**Freak Out**	*When someone becomes irrationally upset or angry, sometimes to the point of confusion.*
96	**Get Ahead**	*To become successful in the professional environment or make consistent progress in life.*
97	**Get Away**	*To escape from something.*
98	**Get Back**	*To return to a place.*
99	**Get Back At**	*To get revenge.*

100-111

100	**Get Back To**	*When you talk to someone at a later time either because you are busy or you have obtained additional or new information.*
101	**Get Behind**	*To learn, work, or progress more slowly than others.*
102	**Get By**	*To pass someone or something.*
103	**Get Down**	*To move to a lower place or level.*
104	**Get In**	*To arrive or enter a place, room, building, etc.*
105	**Get Off**	*To leave a form of transportation, except a car.*
106	**Get Off On**	*To be excited or to truly enjoy doing something.*
107	**Get On**	*When you move your body and either stand, sit, lie, kneel, etc. towards something (non-separable).*
108	**Get Out**	*To leave or escape.*
109	**Get Over With**	*To finish something that needs to get done.*
110	**Get Through**	*When a message, meaning, or idea is understood or accepted.*
111	**Get To**	*To arrive to or assist someone to a place.*

112-122

112	**Get Together**	*To meet and spend time together.*
113	**Get Up**	*To move to a higher level/position.*
114	**Give Away**	*To give something for free or without expecting anything in return.*
115	**Give In**	*To surrender to something.*
116	**Give Out**	*To distribute something.*
117	**Give Up**	*To stop doing something without completing it.*
118	**Go About**	*To take the necessary steps to get something done.*
119	**Go After**	*When you do your best to get something no matter how difficult it is.*
120	**Go Ahead**	*To proceed to do something that you were hesitant about.*
121	**Go Around**	*To follow a circular path.*
122	**Go Away**	*To move or travel from one place to another place.*

123-133

123	**Go Back**	*To return to a place, time, activity, or a person.*
124	**Go Back On**	*When you fail to fulfill a promise you made to someone.*
125	**Go Beyond**	*To be more than or better than what is normal or expected.*
126	**Go By**	*To pass someone or something quickly.*
127	**Go Down**	*To move to a lower position, place, price, level, etc.*
128	**Go For**	*To try to obtain.*
129	**Go In**	*To enter a place, building, room, etc.*
130	**Go Off**	*To leave unannounced.*
131	**Go On**	*When something takes place.*
132	**Go Out**	*To leave a place or area you're in.*
133	**Go Over**	*To review something.*

134-144

134	**Go Up**	*To move or extend to a higher level or farther North.*
135	**Go With**	*To accompany someone to a place.*
136	**Goof Around**	*To waste time doing silly or unimportant things.*
137	**Gross Out**	*To be disgusted with someone or something.*
138	**Grow Out Of**	*To become too big or too tall for your clothes.*
139	**Grow Up**	*When you physically change from a child to an adult.*
140	**Hand Back**	*When you return something to the person who owns it after the person has given it to you*
141	**Hand In**	*To give something to a person of authority.*
142	**Hand Out**	*To distribute something free to other people.*
143	**Hand Over**	*To give upon request or demand.*
144	**Hang Around**	*To spend time in a place or an area.*

145-155

145	**Hang On**	*When you hold something, often for support of comfort.*
146	**Hang Out**	*To hang something, usually wet clothes, to dry.*
147	**Hang Up**	*To hang clothes or an object on a hook, hanger or rod.*
148	**Have On**	*To wear clothing, cosmetics, perfume, etc.*
149	**Head Back**	*To go to a place where you've been before or where you started from.*
150	**Head For**	*When a situation becomes more likely.*
151	**Head Toward**	*To move in the direction where someone or something is.*
152	**Hear Of**	*When you learn about something or someone.*
153	**Heat Up**	*To make something warmer or cause a rise in temperature.*
154	**Help Out**	*To assist people with something.*
155	**Hit On**	*To suddenly have a solution to a problem or an interesting idea.*

156-166

156	**Hold Against**	*When you don't forgive or have little respect for someone because of something they did.*
157	**Hold Off**	*To delay something.*
158	**Hold On**	*When you wait for a short time.*
159	**Hold Out**	*To extend your hand or an object in front of you.*
160	**Hold Up**	*To hold someone or something up in the air.*
161	**Hook Up**	*When you connect two electrical devices together.*
162	**Hurry Up**	*To do something quickly.*
163	**Keep At**	*To continue doing an activity even though it may be difficult.*
164	**Keep Away**	*To avoid getting close to someone or something.*
165	**Keep Down**	*To make sound, music and noise minimal.*
166	**Keep From**	*To stop yourself or other people from doing something.*

167-177

167	**Keep Off**	*To avoid discussing a particular subject or topic.*
168	**Keep On**	*To continue doing something.*
169	**Keep To**	*When you don't share information.*
170	**Keep Up**	*To continue to do something.*
171	**Kick Back**	*To illegally pay extra money to someone as part of the price.*
172	**Kick Out**	*To force someone to leave an organization or place.*
173	**Knock Off**	*To use force to cause someone or something to fall from its place, whether intentionally or accidentally.*
174	**Knock Out**	*When someone is struck hard enough to cause them to lose consciousness.*
175	**Knock Over**	*To make contact with something or someone in such a way it or they fall.*
176	**Know About**	*To have knowledge of or be familiar with something.*
177	**Lay Down**	*To place something on a surface or an object.*

178-188

178	**Lay Off**	*When a company or business ends a worker's employment.*
179	**Lead Up To**	*When a period of time or a series of events cause an event, situation or conversation to happen.*
180	**Leave Behind**	*When you don't take something or someone with you when you leave.*
181	**Leave Off**	*To accidentally or intentionally not include a person or thing on a list.*
182	**Leave Out**	*To not include someone or something.*
183	**Let Down**	*To disappoint someone.*
184	**Let In**	*To allow someone or something to enter a place.*
185	**Let Off**	*To allow someone to leave a car, bus, train etc.*
186	**Let On**	*To tell something that is a secret or private.*
187	**Let Out**	*When you give permission for someone to leave or be released from a place.*
188	**Let Up**	*When someone or something becomes less intense or strong.*

189-199

189	**Lie Around**	*To be lazy or to not do anything.*
190	**Lift Up**	*To raise someone or something to a higher level.*
191	**Light Up**	*To illuminate something.*
192	**Lighten Up**	*When a conversation is changed or a person changes to become less serious.*
193	**Line Up**	*To form in a row one after another or side-by-side.*
194	**Live With**	*To share the same residence.*
195	**Lock In**	*To secure people or things behind a closed door.*
196	**Lock Out**	*When you don't have the key or passcode to enter a secured place.*
197	**Lock Up**	*When you shut the windows and doors of a place or building.*
198	**Look Around**	*To turn your head to see what or who is around you.*
199	**Look At**	*To divert your eyes to someone or something.*

200-211

200	**Look Forward To**	*To anticipate a future event because it either makes you happy and/or you benefit from it.*
201	**Look Into**	*To investigate or get more facts about something.*
202	**Look Out**	*To remain alert.*
203	**Look Over**	*To examine or inspect something or someone.*
204	**Look Up**	*When a situation becomes better.*
205	**Look Up To**	*This particular phrasal verb is used to say you view someone with respect and/or admiration.*
206	**Make For**	*To go in a certain direction, typically in a hurry.*
207	**Make Of**	*To understand the meaning of something.*
208	**Make Up**	*To invent a story.*
209	**Mess Up**	*When something is dirty or unorganized.*
210	**Mix Up**	*To put or combine different things together so they'll merge successfully.*
211	**Move In**	*When you bring your personal belongings and stuff to a new place where you will live. Yesterday's phrasal verb, Move Out, has the opposite meaning.*

212-222

212	**Move Out**	*When you permanently remove all your belongings and personal items from a place where you live or stay.*
213	**Narrow Down**	*To reduce the number of options or possibilities.*
214	**Pay Back**	*When you return money that you owe someone.*
215	**Pay For**	*To purchase merchandise.*
216	**Pay Off**	*To repay money that is owed to a person or entity.*
217	**Pay Up**	*To pay all the money that is owed or asked for.*
218	**Pick On**	*To tease and/or criticize someone over a period of time.*
219	**Pick Out**	*When you are able to recognize something or someone from a group.*
220	**Pick Up**	*To get someone or something from somewhere.*
221	**Pile Up**	*To put things in a pile or heap.*
222	**Piss Off**	*[Informal] To be angry about something.*

223-233

223	**Plan Ahead**	*To prepare for a future event or situation.*
224	**Plan For**	*To prepare for a big event or expectation in the future.*
225	**Plan On**	*When you have the intention to do something.*
226	**Plug In**	*To connect an electrical device to an electrical outlet.*
227	**Plug In/Into**	*To connect an electrical appliance/machine to another piece of equipment or to a power source.*
228	**Plug Up**	*To block a narrow passage such as a hole, drain, or pipe so that nothing can flow through.*
229	**Point Out**	*To make someone aware of something.*
230	**Point To**	*When you aim at something or someone using your finger or hand.*
231	**Pull Off**	*To succeed in doing something difficult or tricky.*
232	**Pull Over**	*To drive your vehicle to the side of the road to stop.*
233	**Punch In**	*To enter data or record time on a device.*

234-244

234	**Punch Out**	*To record the time you leave the workplace using a special clock.*
235	**Put Away**	*To place something where it cannot be seen or isn't in the way of other things.*
236	**Put Back**	*When something is causing a project to slow down.*
237	**Put Down**	*To place something on a surface or an object.*
238	**Put In**	*When you invest or make a deposit. In this example, the amount almost always separates the verb.*
239	**Put Off**	*To become offended by someone or something.*
240	**Put Out**	*To extend a part of your body.*
241	**Put Past**	*To not be surprised by a person's actions. [Always used with the negative]*
242	**Put To**	*To cause someone or something to be in a certain state or to do something extra.*
243	**Put Together**	*To assemble or connect the parts of something.*
244	**Put Up**	*To move an object to a higher level.*

245-255

245	**Put Up To**	*To encourage or persuade someone to do something.*
246	**Put Up With**	*To tolerate or accept something that you'd rather not.*
247	**Ring Up**	*To call someone on the phone.*
248	**Rip Off**	*When someone asks for a price for something that is too high, when someone cheats or steals.*
249	**Rip Up**	*To tear something (i.e. paper, cloth, etc.) into pieces.*
250	**Rule Out**	*When someone or something is excluded as a possibility.*
251	**Run Across**	*To move or run from one side to the other.*
252	**Run Around**	*To go from one place to another in a hurry.*
253	**Run Down**	*To hit someone or something with a vehicle.*
254	**Run Into**	*When something collides with another object by accident.*
255	**Run Out**	*When people exit a place very quickly. Run In/ Run Into is the opposite of this meaning.*

256-266

256	**Run Over**	*When someone is injured or killed by a vehicle.*
257	**Run Up**	*To run from a lower elevation or level to a higher elevation or level.*
258	**Screw On**	*To ensure the top of a container/bottle is sealed.*
259	**Screw Out Of**	*To cheat or deceive someone.*
260	**Screw Up**	*To make a mistake or do something really bad.*
261	**See About**	*To seriously think about doing something.*
262	**Sell Out**	*When all the inventory of a particular product has been purchased.*
263	**Set Up**	*To organize or plan for an activity/event to happen.*
264	**Settle Down**	*To begin living a stable and routine life.*
265	**Settle For**	*To accept something even though it's not what you want or need.*
266	**Shake Up**	*To mix something in a container by shaking it.*

267-277

267	**Show Off**	*To overly display your skills or what you have.*
268	**Shut Off**	*To stop the operation of an electrical or mechanical device.*
269	**Shut Up**	*To stop talking.*
270	**Sign In**	*To write your name on a list to indicate the day and time you arrived at a certain place.*
271	**Sign Out**	*To write your name on a list to indicate the day and time of your departure.*
272	**Sit Down**	*To change from a standing to a sitting position.*
273	**Slow Down**	*To do something slower.*
274	**Sneak Out**	*To leave a place without being noticed.*
275	**Space Out**	*When someone's attention is not in the present moment. [Adj.] {spaced out} To describe a person whose attention isn't in the present moment.*
276	**Stand Around**	*To stand in one place or area when you should be doing something.*
277	**Stand For**	*To support or represent an idea, belief, etc.*

278-288

278	**Stand Up**	*To rise from sitting or lying down to a vertical position.*
279	**Start Out**	*To begin a trip or venture to some place.*
280	**Start Up**	*To start something.*
281	**Stay Off**	*To avoid discussing a certain subject or topic.*
282	**Stay Up**	*To remain in a place that is higher than ground level.*
283	**Step On**	*To place your foot on something or someone.*
284	**Stick Around**	*To stay in a place or with someone for any period of time.*
285	**Stick Out**	*To extend something outward.*
286	**Stick To**	*When something is attached to another by some form of adhesive.*
287	**Stick Up**	*To use a weapon, especially a gun, to rob someone.*
288	**Stick With**	*To continue to use or do something.*

289-299

289	**Stop Off**	*To make a quick stop on your way to a destination.*
290	**Stop Over**	*To visit someone for a short period of time.*
291	**Straighten Out**	*To make something straight.*
292	**Stress Out**	*To feel very worried, nervous or anxious.*
293	**Take Apart**	*To disconnect or separate the parts of an object.*
294	**Take Back**	*To return something or someone.*
295	**Take In**	*To be successfully tricked or deceived by someone.*
296	**Take Out**	*To remove an object from an area, place or container.*
297	**Take Out On**	*To direct your anger towards someone or something when you're really upset about someone or something else.*
298	**Take Up On**	*When you accept an invitation or offer from someone.*
299	**Talk Down To**	*To talk to someone as if they are less intelligent than you by conveying a tone of voice or attitude that says so.*

300-311

300	**Talk Into**	*To convince someone to do something.*
301	**Talk Out Of**	*To convince someone not to do something.*
302	**Talk To**	*To have a conversation with someone.*
303	**Tell Apart**	*To be able to differentiate something or someone from something or someone else.*
304	**Tell On**	*To inform an authoritative figure about what someone else did.*
305	**Think About**	*To consider something prior to making a final decision.*
306	**Think Ahead**	*To think and plan carefully for a future situation or event.*
307	**Think Up**	*To use your imagination to create a plan, idea, or a solution.*
308	**Throw Away**	*To dispose of something, you no longer find useful in a waste bin, trash, etc.*
309	**Throw Out**	*When you get rid of something by putting it in a trash can, bin, etc.*
310	**Throw Up**	*To vomit or puke.*
311	**Trade In**	*To exchange something old for something new.*

312-322

312	**Trick Into**	*To convince or persuade someone to believe something untrue or to do something for you.*
313	**Try On**	*To see how something fits or looks before purchasing.*
314	**Try Out**	*To show that you are qualified to do something.*
315	**Turn Around**	*When someone or something moves until it faces the opposite direction.*
316	**Turn Down**	*To decrease the temperature, sound, etc.*
317	**Turn On**	*To cause someone to feel interested and/or attracted.*
318	**Turn Out**	*To attend an event, meeting, etc.*
319	**Turn Over**	*To move an object so that the part that is on top becomes the bottom and vice versa.*
320	**Turn Up**	*To increase the controls of an electronic or mechanical device.*
321	**Use Up**	*To completely consume or use all of a supply.*
322	**Wake Up**	*When you are finished sleeping.*

323-333

323	**Wash Off**	*To remove dirt or unwanted markings with soap and water.*
324	**Wash Up**	*To clean your face, hands, body, etc.*
325	**Watch Out**	*To be aware of someone or something.*
326	**Wear Down**	*To make the surface or top of something disappear due to friction.*
327	**Wear Off**	*To decrease or disappear gradually.*
328	**Wear Out**	*When something is damaged or weakened from use and age.*
329	**Wipe Out**	*To clean the inside of something.*
330	**Wipe Up**	*To remove liquid from a surface using a sponge, towel or cloth, etc.*
331	**Work In**	*To make time in a busy schedule for a person or an activity.*
332	**Wrap Up**	*To cover something with some kind of special paper.*
333	**Zip Up**	*To close an item that has a zipper.*

About the Author:

**Coach Moin Khan is an Author,
A Success Coach and a Master Trainer,** he is also the Founder and Chief Mentor at **Amazing Institute of Training and Development.**

He has Trained, Coached guided more than 35 thousand people in his 21 years of Professional Training Career.

He has trained people from more than 35 Countries. He Specialises in the field of Public Speaking, Body Language, Communication, Training and Success Coaching.

His Mission in life is to help 1 billion people unstuck from their Limited Mindset, unleash their True Potential, have more Clarity and Courage to move ahead to live the life of their dreams.

www.theamazinginstitute.com